RANDOM HEART POETRY

LIGHT AND SHADE

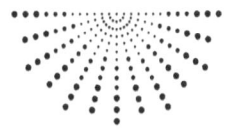

MALA NAIDOO

Copyright © 2020 by Mala Naidoo

All rights reserved.

No part of this poetry book may be reproduced in any form or by any electronic or mechanical means, including information storage and retrieval systems, without written permission from the author, except for the use of brief quotations in a book review

Naidoo, Mala

ISBN: 978-0-6484854-7-6 (Print)

ISBN: 978-0-6484854-8-3 (ebook)

ABOUT THE AUTHOR

Mala Naidoo is an Australian author. She has worked as an educator in Australia and in South Africa during the grip of apartheid atrocities and the early days of its dismantling. Mala Naidoo upholds *justice for all* in her novels and poems on culture, race, gender, and identity. Her writing centres on, i*n our angst and joy we are ONE under the Sky of Humanity*

Also by Mala Naidoo:

Across Time and Space

Vindication Across Time

Souls of her Daughters

Chosen Lives

What Change May Come

Life's Seasons - A Collection of Short Stories

For my beloved family, cherished friends and colleagues who have stood by me in the light and shade of life

1
WOMEN

SHE IS WOMAN

Grandmother of generations
Mother of life
Daughter who carried forth
The candle Divine
Sister who cried with us
Girlfriend forever there
Wife of the wilful
Granddaughter of Grace
Lighting a star-laden sky
Basking in maternal warmth
Drawn from eternal strength
Touched by compassion
Serene and ceaseless
She is woman
Carrying hope beyond time

MAMA AFRICA

Dewy mornings, hot days, warm nights
Lush rolling hills and starry skies
Graceful impala, giraffe and springbok
Adorn the landscape

Down in the valley smoke
Trickles atop a thatched roof
Eyes open to sun's rays
Pap bubbles on a coal stove

With a rainbow scarf
Swirled to crown her head
Her long swishing gown
Caresses her ankles

She hums the song of motherhood
Body swaying in rhythm

To soothe and protect
To love and support
To nourish and grow
Her babies too adorn the landscape

2
SYMBOLS OF LIGHT

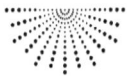

SALT OF THE EARTH

Dark shadows light up
In a heavenly promise
Withered winter leaves
Spring forth in radiant splendor
Snowy acres melt into the earth

The locked soul's key
Rests with self-love
For who will love thee
Without the light of self-love?
Love orbits where love shines

Honor the salt within
To be cherished in return
Nature's resilient child
Springs back to life
Lit in the blood, bone and salt of the earth

DIMINISHED

(FIRST PUBLISHED AS 'LIGHT WITHIN' IN A SPARK OF HOPE VOL 11)

Crushed by the immoral conduct
Of untold hostile human attitude
I retreated into dark solitude
Where the safety of diminished light
Was a promised refuge ever so slight

Then in the silence of that space
I heard these words whispered across my face:
'You are a child of the universe
Listen not to those who curse
For hidden deep are glittering gems'

Like an astronomer scanning the galaxy
To find a host of unseen stars within
Hidden under self-thickened skin
A vulnerable soul they said, is endearing
A newborn babe with innocence peering
Into the depths where a silent light shines

KNOWLEDGE

(Inspired by Plato's Cave)

Search within but hear the call
From yonder expanse beyond the wall
Wisdom beckons from the light
Echoing ignorance as human plight
Go—seek—find and learn the world

Shadows in those infant years
False comfort among growing peers
Never allowed a peek
A desire—a light beyond the wall to seek
To hear—to see—to love and know

The flesh, the mind and soul
Such delights once lost in a dark hole
Stolen from curious sight
The cave of birth a light denied
Now a life of wisdom — secure within

BURN BRIGHT

Inner light burns bright
When drawn from a good kind deed
Shared with those in need

For what can be gained from envy
A heart and soul riddled with hate
Was not created as human fate

Reach out and open heaven's door
Let others feel the sun
To burn bright in shared fun

FLEEING LIGHT

Life is a passing light
Fleeing swiftly from sight
In the rush for much

See beauty around
Absorb the synergy
Of life's energy

Smell the fragrance of nature
The aroma of home's
Simple pleasures

Feel the love, pain and joy
Of all around you
Reach out with compassion

Touch a leaf, hug a child
Hold the old woman's hand
Pat a pet with gentle care

Life is a passing light
Catch its sight
Feel its joy—touch its soul
Live it to the fullest

Tomorrow's light is unsure

OCTOBER BEAMS

Filtered beams of sunlight
Ignite my tired sight
Finding a way to delight
Late on a spring afternoon
And leaves all too soon

Then sunrise looms
When birds stir from night's gloom
To the fresh fragrance of a bloom
Awake in chirping pleasure
Accepting the end of sleep's leisure

With a flurry of activity
The energy of life's synchronicity
Bathes, feeds and prepares to extract
Joy from sunlit beams
On its way down—peeping through blinds

3
HAIKU 1

MOONLIGHT

Diana how radiant thou art!
Draped in silvery cloud wisps
Looming before the winter solstice

HIM

I stared at this face
Wondering at his beauty
Confused I slapped him

(*written aged 15*)

LIFE'S SHORES

On the shores of life
The ebb and flow in rhythmic
Caresses reach out

Tickling feet and toes
In sensual provocation
Dreams on sun-soaked sands

CAR WASH

In seclusion now
Cascading, dancing soap suds

Squirt, splash, jive, tumble
Mind in tune meandering

DAYLIGHT

Daybreak ends night's sleep
Sweet children awake joyous
In nature's embrace

4
AUSTRALIA

IN HOPE

One day beautiful and bright
The next, a raging fire storm
Lightning bolts traveling
Testing selfless firefighters
Battling through the night

Charred remains—many lives lost
Color blackened by the voracity
Of leaping, frenzied flames
Running wildly in wide open spaces
High winds fan hungry flares

Land of the golden wattle
Emu, kangaroo and koala
Once in a blue eucalyptus haze
A land of vast coastlines wide and deep
God's country under nature's blaze

Raise your hands for reprieve this day
For human lives, fauna and flora
To have a chance, a second life
To breathe clear air and bathe in
Crystal clear waters once again.

FIRE

Fire rose by day
Swallowing light and clean air
Silent voices cry

Taken by harsh flames
Memories in burnt ash lay
Silent voices cry

Endurance tested
Under nature's wrath
Silent voices cry

Drenching rain needed
To quench an arid homeland
Silent voices pray

RAIN

Rain has come to douse
The flames upon our house
On the land we call home
A place we call our own
Where in diversity we stand
Rallying together—a band
One world—one country—one people
Fighting for the right to thrive
Survive and stay alive
Calling for climate change!
To ensure earth's global renewal
For generations to come, to know
The beauty of the land we sow
In this our hallowed home

5
LOVE AND LIFE

BROKEN

It takes two to tango
That's how it begins
Attentive, caring, hanging on
The years roll on, children come along
A gradual shift in gears
Too many nights in tears
Questioning: How did it go wrong?
When it was good it was a song
Now hostile aggression jeers
What happened to the vows?
Were they not meant to last?
Empty promises and fading ink
Years given years taken
Searching for a new beginning

THROUGH IT ALL

1982—thirty-seven years gone by
Joy filled my young heart then
To be with my love
My eternal soulmate

We weathered the storms of life
Came out strong side by side
In this woodland called life
Where many struck an unfair blow

Giving was all we ever did
Innate in both our soulful beings
Yet misjudged tossed and turned
But love carried us through

Then illness struck out of the blue
Shook the wind from both our sails
But with you standing by my side
You brought me through the valley

Together we work every day
Growing stronger and better in every way
In a rare union unmatchable
We have love aplenty, and kisses many

VOW

First the courtship
Fluttering hearts and sweet smiles
Holding hands in a permanent clasp
Endless dinners willing time to stop
Beach walks and hugs in the rain
Snuggling together at the movies

Then the vow till death do us part
Children seal the love and joy
Years roll on in family gatherings
Vacations at the beach and festive
Times together wrapped in warmth
Timeless vows in living the promise

Decades pass and children leave
The family fold to find a life
They're destined for
Then with an empty nest and
Vacations for two — a couple

Regains the first flush

Endless dinners long walks
Animated conversations
Planning the next family celebration
The vow of commitment forever there
In eternal togetherness
Pledged

TWO SOULS — ONE LIFE

Two souls in marriage unite
Sharing and learning together
Family first their treasured thought
Then serving community and those in need

Spiritual and humane in every way
Role models in what they do and say
Looking for the best in friend and foe
Never judging or spreading woe

A lifetime in strength together they grow
Sixty wonderful years of love to show
Blessings sent to keep you safe
Happy and loved in every embrace

Longevity assured for marital bliss
When sealed with a heavenly kiss

6
FAMILY

MAMA

A little frame and a curious mind
Reading long into the night
Devouring books at the speed of light

Swift and deft of foot is she
Moving with the graceful ease of flight
Multi-tasking and forever bright

A selfless nurse in her day
Voluntarily serving many forsaken
By a system with equality taken

Ready to bring wellness
To body, mind and soul
When incapacitation was a begging bowl

PAPA

86 today and full of smiles
Lived through untold miles
Of life's strife
To give our family a life
Of love warmth and lack of need

Nothing was ever too much
Putting family first in all you touch
A life lived selflessly
By the grace of blessing
From a benevolent divine

Yesterday today and forevermore
The lessons learned as a child
Standing tall with passion wild
Living your example in justice for all
By bringing down the dividing wall

Peace on earth and good health
Is all you desire as the body's wealth
To serve to grow and nourish
The eternal garden of life

DAUGHTER

When I looked into your eyes
For the very first time
Our eyes locked
Mine on the beauty of your face
That over-swelled my heart's space

The freshness of new skin
The unfurling of little fingers and toes
Downy shiny black hair
Smooth on your delicate head

Then as days passed
My heart lurched with your
First smile
First tooth
First word
First step

Now we laugh late into the night
Your smile wide your eyes bright
The first joy now endless
In a mother's love is ceaseless
That nothing can compare

LIFE'S SOUL-MATE

Silent and still
Few words spoken
A rock in my needs
Sharing laughter
On the things we enjoy

Give and take
Two unlike souls
Finding common ground
In togetherness
In helping those in need

You have your space
And I mine
In respectful celebration
Of our individual calling
Steadfast and light

Supportive, kind and caring
I could not ask for more
In silent stillness sometimes
Finding each other
Extending youth in our golden years

WRITER'S FACE

Yesterday I looked behind
Searching deep inside
To find a forlorn face in the dust
Strange and unrecognized

Fearful then of what I had to bear
Today sounds a different note
Elevated with joy for all I write
And all who have become so dear

And tomorrow invites reflection
On a time plagued by distraction
But blessed smiles nod at life's thrum
A celebration of what has come

Now to turn the grateful face
In humility for being touched by grace.

7
HAIKU 2

BUSH FIRE

Engulfed in red flames
Cremated earth lying bare
Teardrops fill sad eyes

SPRING

Season of wonder
With fragrant morning blessings
The promise of life

LONE ROSE

Lone rose deep and strong
Radiant in morning light
Sharing your beauty

BIRTHDAY

Birthdays were milestones
In the childhood years of life
Now each day matters...

MIST

Rolling twirling sheets
What goes there in the shadows
Eyes wild with wonder

8
RANDOM HEART

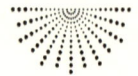

FRAILTY

Every person has a struggle
A life of challenges to juggle
Family first is the call
For a while work consumed all

A careless word or judgement
Has no room in readjustment
Longevity desired is a gift from above
To be respected with care and love

Recklessness in the world abounds
Where a blind eye makes a battleground
Of frailty's need of care
Shut the lid on your despair

For the infirm are at your mercy
Reach out with grace and courtesy

SIMPLE HEART

Love's full heart
Gives and receives
Respect and friendship
United in partnership

Love knows no boundaries
When shared it
Glows and warms
In cherished togetherness

Love's breath and desire
Live the eternal fire
Cradling a life ignited by love

Love reaches out
Spreads arms and opens doors
Invites in those who know not
What love is—let love lead the way

NEW LEASE

Birthday led her to death's door
Came with no warning
To claim some strange score

The universe ordered—not now!
There's much to complete
Don't challenge her vow

The sun shone down to heal
For she has much to do and see
That nothing can steal

As after birth, one step at a time
She's learning a new way
In her quest for the grand design

Grateful is she for the blessing
Of a life she is addressing

HEALING

A life worth living
Is one that's giving
Amid the turmoil
And need to survive
Turn not the eye inward
Pushing others outward

Stop refresh think
How the power of ink
Reaches out to touch a life
Lost in strife and struggle
Wandering through earth's rubble

Stories of survival and hope
Help others in distress cope
Create those wands of magic
To save a life that is lost and tragic

RENEWAL

Divine creation
Beauty in ovation

Heaven and hell in a storm
Ravage earth's form

And with the calm dawn
Hope rises

New life bursts
Forth in glory and
Splendor to beckon
The rebirth of forgiveness

Divine creation
Heals and renews

WINTER MORNING

Frosty mornings
Freezing nights
Winter like clockwork arrives

Jacketed hooded and scarfed
Commuters hunched over
Scurrying to indoor warmth

Mid-morning rays bathe many miles
As glorious sunlight basks
Warming hearts with smiles

Afternoon steals a sinking sun
Grey clouds gather overhead
Cold evening threatens fun

Then fireside reading
Drowsy minds and meandering souls
Conjuring stories for another tale

SUMMER NIGHT

Summer nights
Steal respite
Tossing and turning

Buzzing mosquito
Thirsty disturbance
On a hot summer night

Sweat rises
Thirst unquenchable
Restlessness steals sleep

Broken night
No promise of respite
Sleep denied in heat

Oh gossamer wings of sleep
Infuse this being with rest
On a hot summer night

RESTFUL PONDERING

A quiet hush
Settles over the land
Night closes in
Soft wings flutter
Restless under a dark sky

The bright moon
Stands tall yonder
Its light aglow
Amid dancing trees
Swaying in a gentle breeze

Houses dimmed still
Low breathings heard
As sleep—sweet sleep
On soft downy beds
Claim weary souls in bliss

A SEASON OF GIVING

A blessed season of giving
And sharing of love and care
A time for all seasons

A season of hope and
Abundant joy—oh for the spirit
To be born in all seasons!

In kindness reach out
In prayer, love and be loved
A shared humanity—a union in joy

Songs and blessings
Feasting and gifts

Spare a thought

For the child
Lost in the wilderness

Of poverty and war

A time for all seasons
An eternal bond of love
Always in peace and harmony

No excess, no pricey gifts
Save for the priceless
Gift of love and care.

ON THE HORIZON

Squinting at the orange ball
Fired in the sky of a departing year
Searching in the haze for endless cerulean skies
On the horizon of a new coming
Days passed in pensive mood
Writing upon the pages of life
Passion and fire surging within
Words flowed—lines formed—compositions
   grew

Then unexpectedly in the drama of life
A warning arrived, altering life's course
Passion and fire remain inextinguishable
Slowed pace kept the glow alive
The New Year advances with a promise
Of much to be born on the manuscript of life
Meandering days fill meditative hours
Contemplating embryonic creations

The writer's life comes full circle
At the close of a decade
Filled with hope
On the threshold of a beckoning year

Squinting at a new year approaching
Now sharpened by a yellow sun
In a radiant sky
The joy of life awaits—breathing anew

THINKER

(Inspired by Rodin's Thinker)

What is it you contemplate?
In pensive pondering
With the weight of the world
Stooping your drooping shoulders?

Naked—a babe deep in thought
When ideas flow in a steady stream
Is it climate change, politics
Or abuse of the vulnerable?

That consumes you this way
Can you find the solution
To end war and suffering
For world peace to reign?

Lost deep in thought, gilded with hope
Suspended in timeless ways to cope

WORDSMITH

What will you tell me?
Is there a story
To keep me awake
Under the covers?

Is there a poem
To delight and ignite
My soul and dreams
To set my life aglow?

Is there advice
To guide my pen
To learn your ways
To create my desires?

How do I get there?
Oh wordsmith!
How do I tell my tale
For the joy of my reader?

Across the page
From another realm
The wise wordsmith
Whispers:

Read, oh wordsmith!
Read more
Pick up your pen
Write your story

The reader awaits your joy!

LISTEN

(FIRST PUBLISHED IN SIPAY, DECEMBER 2019)

Hark listen!
To internal desire igniting
The flame of storytelling
Do you hear it—see it—feel it?

Frustration knocked on every door
Hark listen!
Who would answer the cry of the poor?
Voices lost in emptiness

Hope sprung renewed
Words spouted blood on the page
Hark listen!
Desire now alive at every stage

Heart pumping
Words galloping
Hark listen!
For a story is born

SCHOOL'S OUT!

Today will pass in pleasure
Time now for leisure
With no paper pressure

Let's start the holiday
What do you say?
To going out to a play
Take up the offer—not sure?

Then would you like to sing a song
Please come along
To be happy among
Friends we treasure

ON MEDITATION

Stop...settle...still...breathe
Focus...intent...inhale...exhale
Slip slowly down
The open gateway
Down
Down
The light is soft, the air crystal
The sky is blue and clouds dance
Rise like a gentle breeze
Higher and brighter
Above cities, forests, rivers and oceans

Tranquility seeps in through the font
Veins tingle with sensations sweet
Muscles lighten...body weightless
Floating...Flying...Soaring
The visceral chant remains
To greet the day afresh

9
HAIKU 3

MOTHER

Her selfless love gives
Breath to her beloved child
Mother you are life

HEARTBEAT

Pumping blood through veins
Heart falters—night closes in
How did this happen?

THE ARTIST

Artist in Silence
Crafting in Soulful Delight
Touching Many Lives

10
POEMS ON MY NOVELS AND SHORT STORIES

ACROSS TIME

Across Time and Space
Hearts meet, separate
Unite
Longings rise

Time cannot erase desire
Hearts' yearnings
Cannot be stifled

Time heals
Time renews
Space breathes
Space contemplates

Like rain to a drought
Thirst quenched

Life breathes refreshed
Hope ignites the dark skies

Across Time, the void
Of space fades

VINDICATION

Seeking new shores bright and eager
Taking her history hidden deep inside
Paths meet across countries
Indomitable spirits on a quest for justice
    and art

Mysterious stranger brings delight to a lost
    heart
Fate works its charm and challenges abound
Unity prevails when truth is enthroned
Temporary separation and time to think

Four souls—two hearts find their way
To the one destined love
Much happens on the journey to the
    chosen life
Histories collide choices made

Dreams realized in common goals
Crime punished and goodness reigns

SOULS

Untainted souls
Threatened by
Forces beyond sane
Control

Who will save them?
Who will care?

Selfless souls serving
With Passion
Guiding them to
Injured Souls

But who will save them?
Who will care?

Undying, timeless
Love
These are the
Souls of her daughters
Valued, loved, beyond time

CHOSEN LIVES

Noticed, unnoticed
Chosen Lives
Gifts of Humanity
Educate, protect, encourage

Chosen Lives
Gifts of Change
For a New World
Free from pain, poverty and abuse

Chosen Lives
Gifts of Acceptance
Spreading the message
Truth, Understanding, Compassion

Chosen Lives
Gifts of the Earth
Touch the Face of Suffering in Hope
For a New World

CHANGE COMES

For every new season
There's a necessary reason
For change to emerge
With an unexpected surge

Change comes
To happy settled lives
Creating unimagined dives
In the struggle to survive

Change comes
To lead new ways
Whatever the season
No matter, the reason

Fear not the coming
Of dawn's change
The crest of a wave
Will refresh and save

FALLING RAIN

Soft soaking rain
Food of the soil
Fuel for the soul

Come hither gently
To earth's children
Crying out in thirst

Consumed by drought
Life withers
Day after day

Cracked earth, dry dust
Quench the arid land
With a first drop

Come gentle rain
We invoke
Your blessed shower

THE RAIN

(*Short Story Retold in Verse*)

Thuli and Thabo
Mother and son
Vusi and Vincent
Father and son
Baby Gertrude innocent to all
Vincent away working in the city

The family split by the rage
Of relentless rain
Widening the river
Cutting off the village
Days without food

Thuli's pregnant belly
And a song on her lips
Kept her children safe
Until Thabo left

Never to return

Swept away by the
Swell of the river
He knew so well

On Christmas morning
A newborn baby's cry
A family rebuilding
With a sweet lullaby
'Thula tu thula baba'
Hush little baby your
Father's home

11
INDIVIDUAL AND SOCIETY

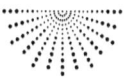

LIFE

Love it or Loathe it
We need it
Can't live without it

Obsession night and day
Texting—Facebooking—Tweeting
Instagramming—Pinterest Pinning...

Give me more
We can't survive without it

We must know
We must see
We must hear
We must play

Fear of missing out

Obsession working

Obsession walking
Obsession talking
Obsession at coffee catch-ups too?

No! Obsession—not when driving...

Sorry officer, I had to...

Book that driver!

IN A NAME

It's a name
It defines me
It defines you

Skin tone—demographic
Dark Brown—Black or White
I am me—you are you

Joy—Love—Anger—Fear
I am me
You are you

Human to the roots
Of my dark or your light hair
I am me—you are you

See beyond—please know me and understand
Dark Brown Black or White
See me—See you—See us

In our angst and joy we are ONE under the sky of humanity

WATCHING... WAITING

I watched from the side
Waiting...
Waiting to be seen...
Wanting to be heard

A Look
A Smile
That says
I See You
I Hear you

A heart cries
I am here...

I'm alive... can't you see?

LAUGHTER ERASED

Where are the children?
Playing in the park
Dancing in the rain
Sitting at the family table

Where are the children?
Around a campfire
Laughing with mirth
Singing with gladness

Where are the children?

Indoors
Computer
Phone
Television

Laughter erased

SEVEN YEARS

Seven Long Years
Torment, Race
Culture, Race
Education, Race

A Ship Sails In
From a Familiar
Shore

Was it a godsend?

Culture—Race—Torment
New shores—old ways

Soul Mates
Steer the Vessel
Through Rocks And
Storms

Seven Long Years
Replaying the Scars

Now Clear Waters
Beckon from a Different
Shore

Seven Long Years
Dip a Toe,
Take the Plunge

Warm Waters
Caress the Soul

Free at Last

MIGRANT'S TOME

Leaving a life already made
Searching new shores for peace
Away from violence and uncertainty
A name already known
On the warm hearth of home

Leaving a life already made
On a quest to expand life's horizon
Away from injustice and sorrow
A name already known
In classrooms and corridors of home

Leaving a life already made
Hoping for a life of many choices
Away from fear
A name already known
To lovers in the shadows of home

Leaving a life already made
Forced on a trek—not from the heart
Away from murder and rape
A name already known
Now a stranger on the cold hearth of home

12
ROMANTIC SPIRIT

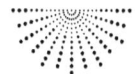

BRIGHT PETALS

Fourteen bright petals arrived
Ready to read, compose, and flourish
Some petals strayed along the way
Sun, wind, frost, babbling brook and rain
Infused those who remained
Rime, Abbey, and Heights
Awakened their Mighty Being
Curiosity, imagination, freedom and nature

But challenged ways of thinking
In a spirit of wildness
Never to be tamed
A celebration of beauty
And self-declared
They dreamed and believed

CREATIVITY

Upon the wings of creativity
Soar like the albatross
Travel in measureless realms

The dipping moon
Throws a passing shadow
Time ignites the morrow

Resilient reaper
The reward beckons

EARTH MYSTERY

Sun scorched fields
Drenched plains
Fires and volcanoes
Lives in jeopardy

But spring elicits a promise
Refreshed to feed earth's
Wide lands with
A sprig—a leaf—a flower

Unfurling in a
Kaleidoscope of color
To blanket heavenly earth
Oh in such glorious splendor!

Birds twitter—bees buzz
As honeyed earth
Hums with the energy
Of promised vitality

LIFE'S BLESSING

(AN ELFCHEN)

Life's
A Blessing
From the Divine
In Gratitude I Give
Thanks

The End

AFTERWORD

Poetry says so much in a few short lines. It is a literary form that enhances all other writing if observed for the depth and clarity it brings. From reading and teaching poetry emerged the inspiration to handwrite poems as they arrived in the conscious mind. Now it's the glue that holds my writer life together.

If you are an aspiring poet here is a blog post I shared on my website:

Poetry Educates Prose

Poet or novelist, one, the other or both — one grows into the other almost instinctively to develop the ideal creative state.

Writing improves with consistency and ongoing learning of the essentials of the craft. The art of writing expands the imagination and bulks the creative muscle by triggering the desire to know more, to research, to read, to push boundaries, and feel joy — a perpetual quest of the writer.

Voracious reading of all forms and more particularly poetry, the fine art of saying much with an economy of words, is a skill worth learning to enhance prose writing skills. Poetry as a literary form is laden with layered sensory imagery, conveying pain and joy, the state of the human condition and a celebration of nature which when emulated in prose fiction, is the *lyricism in narration* or the *cadence of poetic storytelling*.

The habit of reading poetry grows the writer's ability to choose appropriate/effective language or specific words that says it all with brevity. We live in an era where attention span is brief, access is quick, and impatience governs desires.

Little bursts remain to sustain…

There is an intensely intimate, mindful experience apparent

in poetry, a purity that makes it more personal where prose is more social, and when married with a sensitivity to both forms, the reader benefits from the writer's authenticity.

As a teacher, evidence suggests that incremental learning leads to lifelong knowledge. Piecemeal understanding is committed to memory in meaningful short bursts as opposed to lengthy mindless memorisation that disappears after the moment of recall.

Poetry speaks in the rhythm and profundity of its brief lines, a boon in holding the attention of the reader.

Poetry read before sitting down to write prose, or read as the last activity before sleep sharpens the ability to borrow from the poetic form and style for precise, well-formed ideas that touch with the depth and clarity that poetry engenders.

If writing in a particular genre or establishing an emotion in a prose scene, turn to poetry that's appropriate in that instant and feel the passion and power of the words and those left unsaid, then a deepening of thought processes emerge to heighten the imagination. Reading poetry written in any period has the inspirational ability to enhance overall writing.

Crafting poems for creative leisure or publication is beneficial as self-directed editing of what works and what requires reworking. Poetry cannot hide intention and purpose, it's stark, it's true, a visual and emotive painting through words. This skill shapes brilliance in prose writing.

Poetry and prose are close cousins of the writing family. Read as many novels as you would poems, or more to capture that sweet spot of simple, short, stunning sentences, one after the other, until a story is born.

How many poetry books are there on your bookshelf? The internet is a valuable source, but there's much to be said on having a book in your hand as you read, delight in, make note of, absorb and contemplate.

For aspiring writers: Write a poem today on any topic, let it tumble freely onto the page, then try your hand at prose. Watch the magic unfold. An open mind is necessary to attain this joy, and brilliance in prose writing.

If you have enjoyed reading my poems please leave a review on your chosen platform so that other readers might find my random heart and dwell in the light and shade... for a while.

With gratitude,

Mala

www.malanaidoo.com